"The dept
the day o. ___ ___ ___
The Cost of a Flower." In this early piece, we meet an old woman questioning a Russian soldier, "Why are you here? Why are you here?" The soldier's only response is a weak, "I was told this was an exercise." Unlike this naïve or deluded soldier, the old woman recognizes the politically expedient lie he bears with his rifle. Then, "She offers him / sunflower seeds to put in his pocket / so when he lies down in this cold land / flowers will get back up." Is that a germ of hope that Ukraine will rise again in spite of the invasion? Or is it the fatalism of a generation that knows the truth of war?

One of the harshest realities of the war is played out in Bargen's "After the Dam on the Dnieper River." When the dam is blown by Putin's army to "slow the Ukrainian counteroffensive," the floodwaters swallow up the Fairytale Abrova Zoo—a, now, darkly ironic name—and all 300 animals drown. Still, Bargen's lines march on through the ravages of this war.

Walter Bargen's book finishes with an Epilogue of poems that bring the barrage of words and images unsettling our five senses to an uneasy but just close. His unrelenting vision of the seemingly irreversible decimation of all life in war will insinuate itself into the reader's consciousness and conscience for a long time to come. Do not turn away. Keep reading and thinking in spite of the Thought Police that might be lurking in our margins."

- Julie Chappell, author of *Mad Habits of a Life*

Other Books by Walter Bargen:

Radiation Diary: Return to the Sea
Too Late to Turn Back
You Wounded Miracle
Until Next Time
Dancing in the Night Club of God
My Other Mother's Red Mercedes
Too Quick for the Living
Perishable Kingdoms
Three-Corner Catch
Gone West (Ganz im Westen)
Quixotic
Harmonic Balance
Water Breathing Air
At the Dead Center of Day
The Vertical River
Rising Waters
Yet Other Waters
Mysteries in the Public Domain
Fields of Thenar

Orwell at the Kremlin

Poems by Walter Bargen

Spartan
Press

Spartan Press

Kansas City, Missouri

Spartan
Press

Copyright © Walter Bargen, 2024

First Edition: 1 3 5 7 9 10 8 6 4 2

ISBN: 978-1-958182-80-2

LCCN: 2024942303

Cover image: Michael Sleadd

Title page image: Michael Sleadd

Author photo: William Palmer

Acknowledgments

Some of these poems first appeared in the following
publications, sometimes with different titles:

*Another Chicago Magazine, Blue Will Rise Over Yellow-
Anthology, Days Like This Are Necessary – New & Selected
Work (BkMk Press), Hotel Masticadores, The I-70 Review,
MasticadoresUSA, The Missouri Review, Pinyon Poetry,
Texas Assignments, Gasconade Review: No One Sees the Irony*

Many of these poems were first serialized in *Gobblers-
Masticadores*, one poem appearing each Tuesday, edited by
Juan de Cierrillo

Table of Contents

Prelude

Epilogue

We talked of the last war, when
Houses, cathedrals, towns, shacks—
Whole continents went into wreckage.
What fools could do that again.
—W. D. Snodgrass

We are but the shadows of still
More shadowy things.
—Kenneth Patchen

". . . the worst punishment was the memory. Each battle
brought its own apocalypse. The incredible was routine.
—John Laurence

We are frightened, of course.
But what can we do?
We live with it.
You can't say don't shoot!
They have their job.
We have our lives.

—Valentina (age 73)
Vuhledar, February 2023

This book is dedicated to the children, to the mothers and fathers, and to all the people of Ukraine, who are living through and resisting tyranny, barbarism, and oppression that threatens all of us. And to Volodymyr Zelensky, a shining light in all this darkness.

Slava Ukraini

Weather Forecast Same as Yesterday

Remember Clovis, chieftain of the Franks,
of course you do, baptized in 493 AD,
and accompanied by Bishop Gregory of Tours
on ravaging romps through the countryside.
The bishop praised the "general's" divinely-guided
military conquests, while making certain
that the church received its share of the spoils.
When a Frankish warrior swung an ax
smashing a Soissons vase, profitable pillaging
diminished. Days later, Clovis swung
his axe, splitting the man's skull as he shouted,
"Thus you treated the vase at Soissons."

We shall not fail to recall, Charlemagne,
his loyalty to the church unquestioned,
who, when the conquered Saxons refused baptism,
spent a morning beheading forty-five hundred men.
The field of victory too soggy with blood to go on,
sword wielding arms too tired to lift those long blades
one more time. Heads rolled over the grass, as if they
strolled under the earth then surfaced for a last breath.

The Fourth Crusade, a time we can't forget,
always just over the horizon the clanking
of heavy armored men and horses, the rattle
of lances and shields, as they marched
swinging maces across the parched Holy Land.
Unable to take Jerusalem they turned on Constantinople,

center of Christendom, April 13, 1204, destroying
relics, raping and massacring the citizenry,
as if to prove any city and religion will do
when the time arrives for hacking and cleaving.

Centuries later, on Monday, August 23rd,
2005, in the Gregorian calendar,
on "The 700 Club," televangelist Pat Robertson said
of the Venezuelan president, "If he thinks
we're trying to assassinate him, I think
we really ought to go ahead and do it.
It's a whole lot cheaper than starting a war."
Always protecting his swollen coffers
with his frugal calling for more. For the rest of us,
he predicts a meteor strike in Florida
to take care of Disney World's unofficial "Gay Days."

The Elves of Katyn Forest

It started during the night after the burning of many cities.
It started when the soldiers in uniforms the color of miles
of muddy road began the forced march of the defeated.
The mud of the vanquished and the mud of the victors

indistinguishable. Prisoners became guards, guards
    prisoners.
Dressed in fear and exhaustion, no one any longer cared.
It started in a faraway country, decades before, when money
heaped in wheelbarrows was spent on a loaf of bread;

when someone in a palace signed his name in water;
when a cigarette butt on a sidewalk was punishable by
    conscription.
It started in a shirt pocket crowded with rats, in a bowl full
of glass eyes blinking in all directions in a field hospital.

So the long muddled lines drudged into a dark forest
to a strange mumbled cadence—the belch of boots being
    sucked in
and out of mired miles—forty thousand struggling vowels
and rifle reports the only consonants spoken over the dead

guarding the ditches. Soon the forest turned blacker than
its wet pines. For years, the raw upturned earth burst
into small blooms of brass buttons and bones. An entire
    country
stopped breathing. Each year the trees grow more bloated.

A half century later, out of Katyn Forest miles of mud-
   caked
uniforms march. At dust-choked crossroads villagers look
   for
passing cars. The sucking sound, the faint moans, only
   wind twisting
through the gargoyled and onion-domed churches.
   Couples stroll along

rivers, watching their children run ahead. Cottonwoods
   sail
their leaves on the reddening current. The evening grows
   faint;
the sun's pulse anemic on the water. The children shiver,
   listening
to stories of elves who return to retake the country they
   lost.

Malaysia Airlines Flight MH17

A landscape of torn and burned blankets
That can't be mapped. A phantom that must find a body.
A wrist that denies its scars. An arm that claims no
Attachment. An existence that believes in less
And less. At this early hour there is no hour left.

The alarm clock wails down its electronic throat.
Not minutes before the next step,
But minutes before a final step.
Then there's an eruption without a Vesuvius.
A flight without feathers, without wings.

A crash just the same. Bloated suitcases
With the dismembered scattered
Over the Donetsk-Oblast. Only silence left to store
in the crushed overhead compartments,
forever blowing to the east.

February 24th, 2022,
The Cost of a Flower

In the beginning, three-year-old twin girls giggle
and chase each other, playing tag along the underground
Beresteiska Metro rails. They call the relentless wailing
of air-raid sirens muffled by 20 meters of earth
"the cows are mooing again." Their mother says
she won't read them fairytales anymore.

This night the broad bands of blue and yellow
are blooming around the world. Niagara Falls
pounds the boulders at its base
as mist rises in the colors of the besieged.

Two stories of the Roman Colosseum's ancient
Stones and all the way to the top of Calgary Tower,
are wrapped in blue, wrapped in yellow.
From Vilnius to Cyprus, Japan to Australia,
the Eiffel Tower to the Brandenburg Gate,
from the United Nations to the Empire State Building
petals of light shine flower-yellow and sky-blue.

With sunflower seeds in her pockets,
on the corner of an oddly abandoned
suburban street, an old woman
in the grayest of coats, her faded red hood pulled up
as if to offer protection from centuries-old stories
that have returned. She stands in front of a soldier,
his arms folded over an assault rifle,

still fingering the trigger, as she demands to know,
"Why are you here?
Why are you here?" and he finally says,
"I was told this was an exercise."

She again demands, "Why are you here?"
Still fingering the trigger, he begins
to half-beg her to go home. She offers him
sunflower seeds to put in his pocket
so when he lies down in this cold land
flowers will get back up.

Stardom, Drama Theater, Mariupol

There was no queue along the sidewalk. Nothing on the marquee, but in the parking lot a word painted in large white Russian letters over asphalt to be read by those on high, CHILDREN. The streets empty except for a pack of hungry dogs. The century-old building felt lonely, even with a thousand people sheltering inside.

Most everyone was in the basement. Who sat in the plush but worn seats? Who planned to sleep upright? No one waited for the curtains to open. No one planned to applaud. The roar of one hand clapping hurt all their ears. More deafening than the mourning of air raid sirens.

A few adults lay on dirty blankets spread over the concrete floor. It recalled kindergarten, the irrepressible whispers and giggles. Getting away with something so small as not sleeping, so inconsequential, until a deeper sleep exploded and legs kept running as they lay on their backs.

So many stared upward, eyes holding up pieces of roof and a few unblinking stars.

Crushing Darkness/Maternity Hospital

for Irina Kalinina

You weren't old enough to believe in death.
Death did not exist.

Only a madman demands
That you die. But first he has to find you.

Under a crib, strapped in a car safety seat,
In an overturned stroller, limp in a high chair

Your breakfast unfinished.
And farther back in your mother's womb

As she is carried on a stretcher
Across a field of twisted steel

And concrete rubble, past smoldering
High-rise buildings in what was once a city.

Her stomach still bulging with life
Until the next minute, hour, day.

She died, her child died,
His imperial hunger insatiable.

Orwell At The Kremlin

In one corner of Red Square
there's so much to say,
but it can't be the word **war,**
it can't be the word **invasion,**
it can only be a **Special Military Operation.**

Speaking machine gun fast
Can never be fast enough to escape.
So many that were alive leave their bodies
As they walk into the shell-shocked light.

There's so much to consider
As the rubble of Mariupol deepens
Into a dusty amnesia
And bodies are lost forever sinking
Deeper into the shattered concrete and twisted steel
When not buried in shallow graves in front
And back yards, in the medians of streets,
In city parks, where knee-high crosses sprout,
Carved from exploded staircases
Shattered doors and window frames.
They dangle shreds of cardboard
With names that won't last.
Blown away in the next barrage
Or the ink erased by a cold rain
That quickly mixes into blood-red mud.

The old women complain, their shovels
Are too heavy with frozen clods of unspeakable
Syllables. First there's too much to shout
As the smoke and dust choke
Every sense clinging to life.
Then there's too much to scream
And it can't be screamed loud and fast enough
As those shot in the back of their heads,
Hands tied behind their backs,
Wait for us to speak for them.

The savage hours can't be buried
Deep enough. So many last breaths
Out of reach. There is no second chance,
No second helping on Red Square,
Where blank posters are ripped from anguished hands,
Cyrillic shredded and bleeding
Across cobble stones. Ribs, heads, backs,
Truncheoned, a boot's kick for good measure—
Oh, the pleasure of walking on ripe flesh—
Their uniforms and one-way visors obscuring
The grimace of smiles or tears.
Cavalierly cramming bodies into vans,
The blank leaflets and posters so clearly readable,
Held over their heads for all to read:
These white sheets of sleep,
These blank breaths of declaration,
These origami wings of white doves,
These raids on the unspeakable,
This strange snow that drifts deep
Over what can't be spoken.   11

The Right Thing

Evgenia said of her husband, "I love and hate this man
for his incredible integrity. Vladimir Kara-Murza
had to be there with those people who went out
on the streets and were arrested," for opposing the war.
"He wanted to show that you shouldn't be afraid

in the face of that evil and I deeply respect
and admire him for that. And I could kill him!"
Upon hearing the verdict, twenty-five years in jail,
Vladimir Kara-Murza said, I must be
doing something right.

Bushel Basket of . . . .

Sasha Skochilenko swapped supermarket
price tags in the Perekrestok in Saint Petersburg.
The new price of an apple is now the Russian

Army bombing of the Drama Theater
in Mariupol where 1000 women,
men, and children, were hiding.

The price of potatoes is Russian forces
destroying twenty medical institutions
In Ukraine.

The price of vodka is ten million
Ukrainians killed by the Nazis during WWII
And how many will now be killed by Russians?
The price of cabbage is the people
hiding from Russian bombs in the Metro.
None of them are Nazis. Stop the war.

The price of radishes is that her grandfather
did not fight in WWII for four years so that Russia
could become a fascist state and attack Ukraine.

She is arrested, jailed for nineteen months
before the trial where she was declared
guilty of violating Article 207.3

of the Russian criminal code for disseminating
deliberately false information concerning
the Russian Armed Forces. Caged behind iron bars

in the courtroom, reinforcing the animal she is,
she pleads guilty and wants to know why her investigator,
her prosecutor, aren't charged with the same offense,

since, if she had not been arrested and turned
into a world-wide celebrity, only one old crow babushka,
one cashier, and one security guard would know

of her scheme to state the truth and undermine
the state. A fragile-young woman, dwarfed
by the balaclava-clad police, a "Z" painted on

their helmets, surround her in her rainbow-
colored tie-dye shirt. She is sentenced to 7 years
in a penal colony.

It's All Happening At the Zoo

1

For some it ends. Marjan, lion in the Kabul Zoo,

Survived gunfire, guided bombs, neglect,

Starvation, a revenge grenade attack

From an armed fighter who thought

He could domesticate a starving lion.

Ten years earlier, in Kuwait City, the invading army

Barbequed the zoo's sharks and hippos.

Exotic birds were a delicacy. Giraffes

Stared into stoplights before wandering

Cross-eyed beyond the city limits

to die in the desert.

Fifty years earlier, in the Tokyo Zoo,

During the carpet bombing,

Three elephants, John, Tonky, and Wanly,

Refused to eat the poisoned potatoes.

Syringe needles too weak to penetrate their skin.

They starved, and even in death their trunks raised

Forever between the steel bars in a bonsai greeting

To their keeper standing under a rain of bombs.

2

A rusting van rushes along the highway from Kharkiv,

The roads' rough shoulders littered with the grotesque,

Tanks and armored personnel carriers, statuesque bodies

Declaring their final allegiance,

As the driver's four–legged passengers lose their balance,

Rolling over the straw on each careening turn,

Speeding away from the zoo and incessant

Bombardment, shell and missile shrapnel carpets

Cages and pedestrian walkways.

The small gauge train in ruins,

The van passengers stand on hind legs,

The backseat removed, and stare out windows

At a landscape that kangaroos and wallabies,

Mountain goats and pudu-pudus have never known,

Amazed at how fast they can move, not knowing

That they are traveling from one bombed-out cage

To a safer bombed-out cage.

Dead Living

When an old lady dressed in a scarf and thread-thin dress
walks past the wrought-iron gate and asks, *Where are you
  buried?*

She assures that person that the question
arrives too soon, has yet to find a definitive plot.

She could nod her head and say, *Right here*,
after she spits the dirt from her mouth

and scrapes the wax from her eyelids.
Now she can read the latest bulleted graffiti

raked across her body, or just turn back
and walk off into another hurricane of crossfire.

She keeps falling as if there is no rest even at the bottom
of today. She wipes her hands on a ripped apron.

What her hands have done can't be cleaned so easily.
Perhaps she's incapable of defending her final breath

under this Empire's Inquisition where the shovels stay
  sharpened
and the digging never stops. A robed procession walks

past the craters crowded with armored wreckage
that marks each passing station. Her knees

bleed for forgiveness. No one believes the rot-iron letters over the entrance: Forever Makes You Free.

The florist's doubts bloom all around.
One at a time, she picks the petals:

This time, not this time, this time, not this time.
Maybe in the 15th Century, maybe in the 21st .

Coroner Counts to 200

1

A woman in a worn-thin sunflower dress floating in a well

next to a destroyed column of Russian tanks.

A body found on the ninth floor of an apartment building.

A van driver calls to say he can't find the body he was
sent to collect.

A woman enters the empty classroom to report that her
neighbor is dead.

"I understand everything," the coroner said. "We will try
to collect him today."

"Dad, I am too busy." "Yes, everything is OK."

Not enough body bags.

There was little room for sentiment amid the scale of
the task.

Nine bodies were buried in a field nearby. The team is
exhausted collecting bodies all day.

"These were our neighbors," "Here is Uncle Potka from
the building next door and a neighbor

of his. Here is another person he knew from the building
across the street. This man has a bullet

wound. We didn't know him but we found a passport tucked
     into his pants. This elderly woman

had severe diabetes and we tried to take her out of Bucha
     but there was no green corridor.

She died. This man went for a walk with his dog and didn't
     come back. No pathologists

around but it looks like he was shot." In the dirt on the van's
     back doors is scrawled

'200' - the military designation for the transport of the dead.
     Bodies are stacked to the ceiling.

The sky is grey, the rain keeps falling.

2

There's a morgue in the town Boyarka, about an hour's drive
     south.

Before the invasion, the staff at the morgue handled maybe
     3 bodies a day. Most deaths

from natural causes. Since Bucha was liberated, they autopsy
     maybe 50 bodies a day,

80% of which were violent deaths. The morgue, a small
     outbuilding at the back

of a hospital on the edge of town, where Boyarka meets the
     forest.

Two rented refrigerator trucks, both filled with bodies.
    Body bags piled on

the ground beside the trucks, against the nearby fence,
    either side of the morgue entrance

as if storm clouds fell to the ground and needed to be
    bagged.

3

Brothers dig for a brother and an uncle all in one body.
    The one they found was half wrapped

in a shower curtain and a half rotting rug whose design
    neither recognized. The clothes

and jacket weren't what they remembered. Facing a
    month of decomposition, they just weren't

sure. They want to believe he is still alive. They only see
    what they want to see. But then they

notice the body wears shoes and socks as if there was
    still a chance to stand up and walk away

from these vulgar absurdities. Shoes and socks removed,
    they stare at their own feet.

The same 26 bones divided into tarsals, metatarsals, and
    phalanges. They wrote the details

on a torn piece of cardboard and tied the story of a life
    to the big toe.

The brothers are not alone in bringing a body to the
cemetery. Private cars pull up to the morgue

and bodies are brought wrapped in blankets and rugs.
Relatives and friends come searching

for the body of a father for a friend. He had his
passport on his chest crossing the borders

of earth. Schwartzmueller Meitservice truck newly
designated 200.

4

Rows of destroyed homes and places where bodies lay
in the streets for weeks. At the cemetery,

a priest intones the funeral rites over a coffin. The mother
of the dead man releases a lightning

wail. Close by, past the edge of a forbidden forest,
enormous booms sound as unexploded
ordnance is detonated. So many men buried on
Monday, April 11, in a fresh grave

by the road, as if they will be daily passengers when the
war is over. There are no weekends

here. The 200 team keeps working until the collection
of bodies is complete.

Schwartzmueller Meitservice 200 truck pulls up. The
mortician's phone rings.

Back From the Front

Light carves out the shadowy drinkers and addicts
At the S & M Café. The sun's low angle
Casts the slow burn of bitumen souls.
A cheek bone flares at one end of the bar.
A glistening of blond hair flames
Over a shoulder. A knuckle-knotted
Hand grabs the light and throws it back.
For a moment, it sparks on the far wall.
Eyes squint before the bar turns back
To its drinks as the late sun reorders
The firing squad. Lips ablaze with lies
And praise and disorder, all dancing to
the jukebox rhythms and bass thump of bodies.

Park Bench

It doesn't start on the bench in the city park.
There are too many endings to accommodate
With just one beginning beside this path that meanders
Through splintered century oaks. The sunlight sits
So full and comfortable by itself, recovering from
Its eight minute trip across more space
Than anyone can know. Hardly enough time

To sort through ballooning pillars of smoke
That can't run fast enough
To keep the sky from collapsing
Into spasms of erupting earth
That only wants to bury itself.
The concussive impacts leave
Ears ringing back to yesterday

And hands reach for nothing
That can be an answer to all of this,
Leaving a city wondering how long the light
Will last. An old man on a park bench
Doesn't bother to brush off the thick layer of dust
That leaves him ghost-like and wondering
If his grandson will recognize him,

Alone in the broken-hearted air,
Above shattered shadows
Strangled across the ground.
The storks aren't returning to roost

On nest-topped chimneys.
The roofs, the eaves, the gargoyles,
The decaying masonry walls of so many towns

Now scattered across front and backyards,
In streets worn out by centuries of passing armies,
That led somewhere that no one now remembers.
It's not worth arguing over, with every intersection
Blocked by turretless tanks, no one left to point and say
This is the way to the ruin of a quiet city park.
Sit down here with your final breath.

Born Again

Almost too soon to have a name,

Almost too soon to be christened,

Too soon for any kind of vaccine,

Almost too soon to accept anything but the luscious

      Warmth of another body entering your mouth,

Almost too soon for eyes to open and recognize a face,

Almost too soon for a face to be a home,

Almost too soon for the pureed apricots fed with a
small spoon,

Almost too soon to recognize your own cry above

      Other's cries, choking and so much louder,

Too soon to grab the fur of a passing cat,

Almost too soon to understand that you have a name,

Almost too soon for the vocal chords to migrate into
that first syllable,

Almost too soon to know that there is a name for
everything

And without a name you don't exist.

Almost too soon to surrender your pacifier,

Almost too soon for the 109 empty strollers

Arranged in four rows in front of the Lviv

City Hall on a cold March day,

Too soon for the sharp shadows of late afternoon

To step in and lie down

with two stuffed teddy bears.

Attila at Breakfast

The milk carton she grabs from the refrigerator is
Missing its pictures of missing children
As if the Pied Piper had passed through town earlier
Or there wasn't time to take photos between explosions.
Mourning and the accounting continues:
Anhelina playing in the back yard
After a night of missiled fireworks;
Dimitr on the playground dodging stray bullets;
Oresta, too long in her uncle's basement bomb-shelter
Runs out into the middle of a charred street.
Their mother takes one whiff from the open carton
And knows the cow's idle musings have curdled.

She sits down to stare at the dry heap
of twisted stalks of wheat in her cereal bowl.
She sees what was left of a village sacked
and burned days ago. A house smolders.
One cow remains, too skittish to give milk,
Ready to run if fur-clad tanks attack again.
A gray tabby leaps onto the table, hoping
To lap up what's left. Before she can say shoo,
It bounds back to the floor, not knowing
what to do with a village of bones
missing the milk of human kindness.

Socratic Discord

What a glorious morning, the fires out, the smoke nearly
    gone,
another dead philosopher dead again, blown off of his
    pedestal
in the middle of the night and into the next museum
    room where he
leans, undamaged, against a grand piano that's covered
    with chunks of plaster.

Centuries ago, he wandered, mostly on foot, from village
to village accepting whatever lodging,
bed or barn straw, and whatever meager meal
he was offered, or none at all.

The scope of his reach, the range of his scope,
is the language of wheat fields and bottomless skies.
Now so close to the forest, no one walks the streets at night,
knowing and not knowing what Medieval stories lurk there.

So many citizens devoured already.
Everyone still alive knows what he said,
even those who didn't care and never listened closely,
but they know he said something that made more sense

than what these days have been reduced to,
running from doorway to metro shelter to under the stairs
to bumping into the dark. And then the arithmetic
of who can still count and hold out for lesser sums.

The only business still open after months of shelling
and siege, the Agora Café, storefront windows cross-taped,
these X-ed out visions there to slow the stiletto shards
walking the runway of another hour of explosions.

Not for the living, there is no living in these times,
for the alive or the executed, the hastily burned
without mercy, without hope,
without coffee to reawake the clientele.

No half-full half-empty argument here,
nothing and everything revealed at once:
unmarked graves, mutilated bodies
half-buried in fields fertilized with shrapnel,

mines, and longing, randomly plowed by artillery
with nothing better to do than pound dirt.
Even Hryhoriy Skovoroda, the eighteenth century
philosopher, who spoke Russian, Ukrainian and three other

languages, including farmed fields and pellucid skies,
languages that can't find any rest in these museums
at the edge of small towns, this one shelled on May 6th
at 10:50 pm, leaving his three-meter tall statue intact,

but lightly tarnished precariously leaning
into the ruins. Now he must be evacuated,
carried to a safer place that doesn't exist
except in the kingdoms of philosophy.

His headstone's epitaph,
if not already crushed by tank treads, reads,
The world tried to capture me, but didn't succeed.

Holodomor Harvest

The artillery is back demanding too much too loudly.
When they are happy with death, the batteries cough
Up dirt and flames. What every poetic soul fears,
Blaming the earth for this savage pandemonium.
It's the exploding silence that is the enemy.
It's clear that bullet proof vests are not enough
For this life or the next.

It begins and ends in a forgotten snowstorm
Where everyone craves escape from the heat of themselves.
Their eyes closed even as half-frozen flies try to pry them open,
Hoping to see the flakes of other minds fall into deepening
    drifts.

There's always a chance to see things anew.
Forget the ambush along the hedgerow
Between fallow sunflower fields. So quick, so decisive,
Not a moment's hesitation, not another breath.
Surely, it's some kind of joke. Does anyone
Remember the punchline?

The stiff bodies laid out on their backs,
Straight and thin as the furrows that they lie between.
They don't rise above the earth that hems
In their shoulders. What's left to plant in these fields?
Kilometers away, their comrades are burning
The harvest and salting the shell-ravaged
Rows with cluster bombs.

Between 1932 and '33, four million peasant farmers,
Their wheat stolen by a blood-soaked leader,
Died of starvation. Now it has its own Ukrainian name:
Holodomor. In 2023 there are so many
more bodies to collect and replant before the spring
offensive even as the granaries are rocketed.

Disappearance of the Outside

The brick wall of the elementary school has a hole
That wasn't there yesterday.
A crowd gathers on the sidewalk and decides
If it was a 3rd grade student who just couldn't take it any
    longer and squeezed through to the other side.
Inside the classroom, Struwwelpeter is shelved between
Mickey Mouse and Yertle the Turtle. The waste paper
    basket
filled with so many attempts at crayoned fields of sunflowers
and blue skies, overflows and now drifts across the cold
    floor.

The wall too thick for someone so young,
who knows so little patience, armed only
with a kitchen spoon. What's left is anyone's guess.
The crowd's shocked stares try not to see any further in.

Or maybe it was the postman who couldn't find
the mailbox, crushed by a heavy-treaded steel beast.
Or this is just the way to pass secret endearments
to the teacher even if a short ladder
is needed to reach the hole's crumbling edges.

Or was this a grand philosophical statement
of liberation to let the inside out and the outside in,
worthy of Hryhoriy Skovoroda. A classroom open
to the world with the traffic noise always headed
out of town as the hungry machines
hunt hither and thither.

But, at least, what's in can get out
if another shell is lobbed at the school,
if there are any children still holding on
to their final breath before recess
in the dark inside, facing the darker outside
where they can disappear.

Watch Wars

The window is black,
blackened, as sirens wail.
The magnesium star-fall glitter
rattles the panes.

They cower behind quaking walls
as the searing mechanical necks
twist and throats break. They grow
deaf and dare the all-clear explosive night.

Staring out the darkened window,
Their shadowy reflections wear raccoon
masks; the eyes scooped out, foreheads shiny
as if thoughts were the last to decay.

He fills the kettle with water for coffee,
and then lies down again, to slip back into
the curled warmth of her, a warmth
so complete it could be his own.

The water whistles the way bombs
search for homes that will accept them,
and then both are gone.
She says don't go, as if in a WWII movie,

and they are plunged into the steam
of a locomotive's engine, the cold shoving
armfuls of ghosts aside so they can
see the cars lurch forward,

crowded with the faces of the future
staring down through frost-encrusted
windows. He is about to leap
onto the bottom step of the last

passing car--but the kettle's rising pressure
is a second alarm. There are cities
waking to this and counting their own
dead. He returns, and in front of the stove's

black dials he turns one off, as if closing
a bomber's bay doors, and remembers
her plea to return. Her skin radiates,
and he's not slipping under blankets,

though he lifts them, but under her
skin, and soon they are each half
of one sleep. This is not the world's
shape, bed flat, it's round and they roll

apart. He calls headquarters to say he is
in retreat. There is a rash of fear sweeping over
his chest and arms, his body a map
of advancing armies. He looks closer

to see the soundless red explosions.
His skin erupts, and they do not hear
the war as the rest of the country does—
lost in this longing for sleep?

Minute Rice

Passing through the needle's eye:
a neighbor's camel, another neighbor's horse,
the donkeys they ride, centuries, millennia,
wagon loads of lost time drenched in
this morning's blinking dewdrops, yesterday's
smoldering clouds, Catherine wheels
rolled off Medieval assembly lines,
even before there was anyone to notice,
before the fretting, the hand-wringing,
when a full belly was the full measure of a day,
when a feathered spirit stopped the sacrifice,
when dreams were told, foretold, retold,
when fire was the only door open to night.

*

Near the Arpa and Araxes Rivers,
in Echmiadzin, Eduard Kazarian,
violinist in the Yerevan Symphony,
sculpted an intricate score only visible
through a heavy magnifying lens.
His statue of Charlie Chaplin stands in the eye
of a needle, a caravan of circus
animals painted on a human hair,
mountain ranges stretched along a straw stalk.
Each brushstroke added between breaths,
between heartbeats. An Armenian Christian tradition
stitching through centuries of persecution.
To survive was to be out of sight.
To sew the emperor's new clothes
Was nothing new.

*

Midsummer midway, the *Schotzenfest*,
near the Baltic, towns parade
their sharpshooters heavy with medals
and trophies. Mid-evening, cool this far north.
Carnival lights swarm the carousel,
the Ferris wheel. Comet tails smear red
and green light. The swirling music equally
slurred. Barkers hustle in front of every booth.

A thin man stands midway, mid-throng, his display
tray suspended from his neck. He sells
necklaces with small oil-filled vials.
On a grain of rice, he writes
her name and slips it into a blue
liquid, screws the lid tight,
hangs it around her neck. Ten years
later in a jacket pocket, his fingers tangle
in the leather cord. Hanover, fifty years
earlier, threaded through bomb sites,
reduced to the warp and woof of rubble.
The bombs chalked with messages,
with names that repeat themselves everyday.

Fremont's War

Half-buried in a drainage ditch
shortly after the Berlin Wall fell
and the Iron Curtain was pulled back,
At least, that's the story I was told,
though I can't remember who the teller was.

A Peace Corp volunteer was driving
from Krakow to Warsaw wondering if he still
had a job, an assignment, a duty to finish
what he started. He stopped on the shoulder
of the road a little uncertain what it was
he was seeing.

He knew it was a bronze statue
from the size of the head,
the cap clearly belonging to the working class,
the mustache and goatee perfectly trimmed,
the eyes fixated on the future,
confident that nothing would delay or stop him,
that his victory was assured.

He hired a Polish crew with a crane and flatbed truck
to retrieve what turned out to be a twenty-foot
tall statue. He called back to Seattle
to convince friends to invest in a work
of social realism. He was convinced
that a museum would jump at the chance
to own the historic significance.

With a quarter million dollars in donations,
the statue crated, it was shipped halfway round the world
to be unloaded on the docks of Puget Sound.

After the restaurant owner died in a car wreck,
and no one would purchase the statue of Lenin,
no one believing its polished bronze would bring business
to a Slovak eatery in Issaquah. The city of Fremont,
a suburb of Seattle, offered a low concrete pedestal
at a dog's hind-leg bend on Fremont Avenue
where three side streets entangled obliquely.

It stood there for decades in front of a Taco del Mare.
Soon after its placement, Lenin was attacked
with strings of Christmas lights,
Styrofoam snowballs placed in each hand,
a cone-shaped Santa hat to cover his own.
Capitalism sent Taco del Mare sailing into bankruptcy
to be replaced by Psychic Journey, offering Tarot Readings
and Chakra Balancing, spelled out in neon lights
below the Doric Lodge No.92 with the Masonic Symbol
painted on the brick wall above and behind the new business.
Lenin unperturbed in his ever present next step,
until splashed with a gallon of yellow paint
that ran down the wrinkled furrows on the right side
of his trench coat and a gallon of blue paint
running down along the fields on the left side
of his coat. His pace uninterrupted, fingers dripping red.

This ancient tale of conquest and maniacal empire expansion,
a photographer takes a picture of a man pissing
on a giant leg of Lenin in its permanent Fremont home.

When asked if this was a political statement,
the relieved man answered
in a heavy Eastern European accent, *No comment.*

Invasion Vacation

This is how it goes, usually it's not very far,
But it's that time of year to escape the shelling,
When families pack their cars, along with the kids
And a pet or two, close the door to the house,
And head out on the road not wanting
Real adventure, just an attempt to repeat
The previous year's sunburn and mosquito bites.

Their beach ball punctured after a stray bounce
Over shattered window panes that are destined
To become wave-smoothed beach glass.
Sand-blasted towels too gritty to use
To dry off. Almost bored after a couple of days
Into the week-long cabin rental, until flames
Dissolve the walls into a gray ash and the resort
Along the Black Sea is erased, and the car
Becomes indistinguishable from a direct hit.
So relax, stay a couple more days
Until the food runs out and the pillars
of black smoke walk off in different directions
over the horizon.

Botticelli: Yellow, Blue, and Red

So much for a life well-planned.
February 24th three months before diplomas
Are to be handed out, all the classrooms
Blown open to an early graduation.

No one believes this view of forever:
Windowless, wall less, door less, lightless.
Not that lights are needed with so little
To instruct and obstruct after these brutal flashes
Of illumination, darker than any
Medieval alchemist transforming
The defeat of lead into the cold victory of lead.

The hallway's skull cracked open,
Knowledge pouring out in every direction,
Careful walking over the bite
Of broken teeth from windows and fallen
Ceiling tiles. Now unable to close its mouth,
The hallway grimly grins into the sky.

A brief vision of walking on clouds
Cornered in one blasted room of the school.
They refuse to move beyond
This one body and into the lifeless many.

She stands at an unexpected entrance,
Half-smiling, a glowing red blush
Of a full-length graduation gown, hem flowing
over the pedestal of brick and stone debris
that stretches beyond her reimagined lives.

Her bare shoulders offer a life,
her life, a valedictorian life,
calling for classmates to follow her
through three postponed months.

The first dance, a waltz, to commemorate
a Venus voluptuously rising
on an ocean of spent shell casings. She holds
a parchment of rubble foreshadowing
the coming tide of despair.

She steps over a limitless supply
of shattered concrete blocks.
The graduating class with no choice,
ready to take aim at their futures.

Faces Of Mariupol

No seeing the sidewalk
break into a burnt wave,
charred surf of a hard-bitten inner coast
crashing in a spasm
of clods, concrete, and billowing dust.

How space enters between things
that didn't know space,
volumes pouring into minds
that were thinking other
smaller thoughts until the shiver
that erupts into nothing.

What was once solid tumbles
from a strangled sky,
impacting with the deafening
one-syllable speech
of immutable objects.

Glass confetti
from high windows glitter
over smoldering cars.
Windshields, a sharp sleet
that won't melt off the faces inside.

Glass Elevator

There is a brief moment of flaying arms
and legs, as if a fledgling left its nest too early
in this place known as the Land of Dangerous
Windows. Others call it Tall Building Syndrome.
It happens outside, bouncing,
maybe ricocheting, maybe quick scrapes
against twenty story high walls whose windows
are welded shut. No chance for anything
other than descending breakage. Not a chance
encounter with a starling, a butterfly, the annoying
whine of a mosquito begging for blood.
One day the glass mysteriously shatters
and a body passes through into an afterlife.

Or maybe a frantic swan dive into a bottomless pool
until the bottom is a tangle of steel hand rails,
concrete steps, and planters crowded with leafless bushes
surrounded by piles of dirty snow. Down flights of stairs
in a careening, screaming descent. No need to count
contusions and broken bones, the height too great
for anything less. There's nothing more
to be heard from the now newly former
head of the Moscow Aviation Institute.

Or some say it is Terminal Velocity Poisoning,
resulting from catching an incurable case
of defenestration. No known cure to be found
even in India, where the founder of a major
Russian industrial food conglomerate was

found dead, leaving behind a man-sized hole
in a pane of hotel glass. Oddly, preceded
by a prescient close friend, a businessman from
Yoshkar-Ola who suffered a similar fate at the same hotel
three days earlier. Perhaps it was the only
way they could meet, a lover's leap.

It's a crowded field where most of the deceased
leave Rorschach smears of their plans
on sidewalks and streets, on the hood
and roof of parked cars, the evidence always
found inconclusive, though it's clear
across distant borders, these are cases
known as Comrade Death Syndrome.

So many in the first year of war: the now former Director
of the Military Shipyard . . . the former Commander-in-
chief of Ground Forces of Russia . . . the former Head of
the Financial Department at the Russian Ministry of
Defense . . . the Deputy Chief at the Main Directorate
of Russian Ministry of Internal Affairs.
Amid all the shards of glass, all declared suicides
Or accidents. They failed to heed flight instructions
to live and not stray above the first floor.

Kitchen God

Is this yellow the sun chasing a morning
that's racing to stay alive floors above
the steaming debris of neighbors' apartments?

Is it the exploding yellow of a wheat field
ready-to-harvest as the wind shakes seeds loose
promising another fruitful year of dying amid landmines?

Is it the yellow of thousands of sunflowers
stretching to the horizon but careful to stop
and not cross the sinister borders of the living?

Is it the yellow of painted kitchen cabinets and walls
only meant to be seen from the inside
and now glowing amid the dark debris left

in the night, nine floors above the fire trucks,
backhoes, and bulldozers, and then out
over a city that no longer sleeps?

These yellow walls wreathed in smoke
And the harsh shadows of spotlights, desperate
to uncover what's still breathing

as more rooms collapse into
the fuming canyons of memory,
leaving flames to the firemen

who uncoil hoses before the waters of death hisses.
The kitchen balanced in sun's yellow beacon
blazing a warning against the crumbling skull of concrete

as more apartments give up and dive into the abyss.
Crowds gather, their necks craned back,
staring at a bouquet of spindly flowers in a cracked vase,

the dirty dishes wait to be washed.
Doors no longer close. These walls
have never embraced so much sky.

The crowd mesmerized, lost in their refugee lives,
not knowing what to say in their ragged
rage and resurrected fears.

Flooded with the moment that chairs are smashed
against walls, cabinets emptied, too sick
to hold anything back. Tables holding up ceilings

for the few still able to crawl out
from under what's left, until they too
collapse under the sun's

transcendent yellow eye.
The smoldering building begins
to spill secrets over the sleepless city..

Still Life

On their knees, half-closed eyes cast down before the pasty,
flesh-colored wall. Halfway up, a cheaply framed, mother
  and child,
hangs squarely near a jagged fissure in the only wall
  standing.
A new border to cross, to defend, as everyone dies in two
  dimensions.

Behind the jig-saw debris, the town's citizens call out to
  anyone who dares
to walk the street day or night, past what little is left,
  calling them
to enter, to trapeze over the collapsed roof, board on
  board as the day
recalibrates: 105 millimeter, 155 millimeter, 75 millimeter.

Balanced at impossible angles, fractured under
the weight of gray sky,
the splintered rafters crowd the pews
as if this is war's final communion.

A halo surrounds her head and the child's
that she holds wrapped in her arms. The chaos
of silence so deep, how can anyone hear more.
Eyes averted, on broken knees they come.

Track and Field

. . . two vast and trunkless legs of stone . . .

—Shelly

One leg is always jealous,
unable to stand up to what is being asked,
always falling behind, plodding
the downfall of the other.
The amputees know their legs

stand in unknown rooms
in separate bombed out houses
and quickly buried along mined roads.
They limp, fly, crawl,
Are flayed from explosion

to explosion. Divergent directions
for divergent legs walking aimless,
trunkless, into the snow where lives
melt away. Different sized doors
open on the same house

that's not yet rebuilt
or waits to be bulldozed into forever.
Owners that never return.
Arguments between legs wears
the floorboards thin, one leg at a time

they plow ruts in the dirt.
Relentless striding back and forth
to outdistance the phantom pain
between the useless, roofless,
water-stained walls.

Sometimes from the windows.
faces stare out exhausted
in their discreet disbelief.
Another blast breaks the panes.
All that's left are furtive eyes

orbiting stilled heads.
How little balance
in a tilted gait. Furniture shifts
with each unequal step.
Unclear destinations haunt

what comes next. Forget the eyes
in the back of heads, good only
for seeing what's already past seeing.
No way to escape the imprisonment,
the tortured time. A wistful longing

for another day's passing.
Always on the threshold,
each step followed by a ghost step
limping into the past, wanting
to recover a many-legged future.

Field Hospital

One entrance requires
walking on his lips.
Another slams open silence
as darkness pours from his ears
drenching his shredded shirt.

It makes no difference
if the doors are closed,
unbuttoning his habit of days,
his body falls away on both sides.

On the gurney by the sliding doors,
a bullet perches in his pocket,
nests behind ribs in a lung still
burning with shrapnel.

On the other side of the curtain
a creek pressed too hard
into his thoughts
and the valley washed away.

His eyes find the sun
between four windowless walls
that are no longer walls but rubble.

Across last year's ambushes the bones
are collected, polished,
displayed in the halls of upheaval.
In the evening, worlds are in collision
as shadows thunder past.

Their bodies live openly with their secrets.
Sand drifts across the bed.
The floor is never swept clean
of Blake's tiny quartz worlds.
The brass-winged shells tumble
through the tide of an incoming barrage.

They Line Up to Die But Not Yet

Is it these steep-pinched valleys that rush the river
In its precipitous fall through bouldered gorges
Or is it these snow-melt choked rivers that push
These mountains out of themselves,

And with them, conscripts who dare to declare freedom?
Either way or neither way, they gun the engine to make
The grade. Pump the brakes, hoping not to ignite
The over-heated oil and grease that flashes fire over the
    engine.

Here at the border that makes no sense,
This mountain or that one, this ridge or one farther on,
Neither here nor there, but demarcated, fenced in, fenced
    off,
The occasional dismembered mountain goat sprawled
    near the trail,

A warning of what's hidden, what's buried. Mine or yours?
It's here, the road, barely more than one lane,
Frequently blocked by mud and rock slides, snow
    avalanches,
and any car that approaches from the opposite direction.

Once, two cars stopping at the border post
was a full day's work and more than enough
For the guards who forget what they are guarding,
And where their Kalashnikovs were planted,

Sprouting rust and dust in the corners
Of an unheated room until yesterday
When the cars backed up five kilometers.
It all moves so slowly as passports are checked

And searches made for contraband,
Which is the very lives of drivers and passengers.
The guards listen to explanations between
All the lies for crossing into another country:

Visiting relatives, sick or not,
The sudden need for a very long vacation
That will become longer, if not unending,
In a cabin without internet or phone service,

A holiday celebration, wedding of a niece,
A change of scenery, a job interview.
Without a shot fired, an unarmed army
Retreats from the battlefield, car windows

Closed, they are protected by floor to ceiling suitcases
And backpacks, concealing their life's knick-knacks,
Food that won't quickly spoil, packs of cigarettes
To bribe officials at the next border post.

Far back in the idling line a madman grips
The wheel of his empire, a choke hold with bottled ricin,
Small metal caskets of polonium,
Assorted nerve agents, to sweeten tea and underwear,

That now roll back and forth across the car floor
In the stop and go crawling toward the border.

These young men and women line up to die
But not yet. The next town, the next country awaits.

Where the next skirmish, battle, counter-offensive,
Special Military Operation, is being planned.

Quickly Aging Retreat

To say it's raining again today, when it isn't,
is simply to prepare these recruits for the fact of snow
that drifts against fences and over abandoned faces
that could advance no farther toward their objectives.

Snow-smoothed runways for vast winds
and the zipper-sting of cold.   Roads blanked,
as if they'd never driven this way, and now
there is no way out but running across backyards

and fields, leaving a confusion of foot prints
and a Hansel and Gretel trail of abandoned equipment.
The safe room where they curl to thaw their hands,
the flickering yellow light surrounded by so few years left

as the shells of friendly fire whistle over their heads.

After the Dam on the Dnieper River

1

Who has time for this, all the bridges
Wading up to their knees
But can't reach either shore?

If they must cross, they strip off
All their clothes. They are only
A thin disguise to deceive themselves

And soaked through
they will only drag them under.
Forget about the cold.

Just keep kicking and reach for
The next meter of water as if it will
Turn into solid ground.

With luck, the last stroke
Will at least be solid as mud
Allowing them to crawl the rest of the way

Through sniping and crossfire.
Later children will whisper
From the opposite bank

About a river of mud people
Escaping an inferno,
A city reduced to ashes.

The flickering voice of embers
Stutters into deaf darkness as the current
Erodes the expressionless mud from their faces.

2

All the roads are nameless
Except for the occasional sign
Swinging on a splintered post
Holding on to one loose screw.

Which road is it that leads
Out of town in search of its name
That's blown into the next town
Then blown into the next

Until being lost is de riguer.
What's left is cratered footpaths
Where anyone not concentrating on the next step
Stumbles to the muddy bottom, falls

Onto something twisted and sharp,
Cries out for help, or falls on top of someone
Who has given up saying hello. These roads
That parallel the river can no longer

Keep up with the current spinning
And splitting around concrete columns
That once worked so hard to hold up cars
Filled with helium balloons to celebrate birthdays,

Early morning bread trucks making deliveries,
Tankers filled with fresh milk,
Buses dropping off the bleary eyed,
All the daily habits of a city that is no more.

3

August 1941, WWII, the Soviet army blew up
The dam to slow the advance of the German Army.
That would end in the winter

Siege of Stalingrad. Maybe 10,000
Soviet soldiers and citizens
died in the flooding.

In 1943, the retreating German Army
Would blow up the dam to slow
The advance of the Soviet Army.

On June 6th, 2023, the Russian Army
Would again blow up the Nova Kakhova Dam
To slow the Ukrainian counteroffensive.

Just below the dam, three hundred animals
Living in the Fairytale Abrova Zoo drowned.
In the aftermath, TASS news

Reported that the zoo did not exist
Only to later report that the zoo existed
And all the animals were safe.

Minefields were washed away switching
a known danger into an unknown danger.
Salmonella, E. coli, mixed-in

With outbreaks of cholera. Beaches became
Garbage dumps and animal cemeteries.
Ninety-five thousand tons of dead fish

Covered the bottoms of the dried up reservoir.
Half of the worlds population of Mediterrean
Gulls breeding on sandy mid-river islands

Lost their 2023 breeding season.
Over 120,000 acres flooded.
Half the flooded forests not shredded

by manic artillery predicted to die.

Body Politic

1

From his ankle to his toes, back up to his knees,
Hairpin turns everywhere, skid marks across his hips,
Rope burns connecting his fingers, palms,
Wrists, elbows, shoulders, the duplicities
At times overwhelming, at times the inventory
Not adding up, coming up short, at times hacked
Or simply lost, maybe stolen by a drug addict
Or Wall Street investor, buried in the pockets
Of corrupt politicians, no time left to change
Anyone's quaking mind, shot through at a checkpoint.

2

And then the little complications,
From neck to jaw to tongue, eyes and forehead,
All swinging open and closed
With every step, a breezy stroll
And then the slamming shut,
And with every blink, the bright brass explosion
A mote in the corner of a bloodshot stare,
Every hinge of hair creaks,
The brush on the dresser tangled with splinters,
Not coming back to the memories of other days
 not coming back to the fireball celebration.

3

Though rarely out of anger, more neglect,
More wind-driven news bullied against chain link fences,
Followed by enough tripping over curbs and steps,
Beyond gangly and awkward, the doors of his body
Blasted open, off balance, legs from other bodies
 close in, wrap around him.

4

Never firm in the jamb
Or well enough insulated to stop winter drafts
Or tight enough to keep the spiders out
During the summer. More the doors
Of rotting perception where bats fly out
The collapsing airport towers of his visions.
His words knocking on the enamel of his teeth,
His tongue the door that won't close,
Banging on every gust of breath,
Not his own as others lean over him.

5

Even when he knows the door,
Always afraid to find out that no one lives
On either side as it swings shut, locked or not.
No one sits at the table that's crossed its legs,
Hoping for cosmic connections even as the starry
Dynamo grinds to a stop at dawn.

Ç'est la Guerre

It was not his intention,
to sit quietly, hands together resting
in his lap, each holding the other
for comfort and assurance, as if they no longer
were headed in different directions,
as if to convince him of the wholeness of his sitting.

Eyes closed wanting only to be a listener,
reduced to pure vibration, the quivering
inner ears recall that first hint of breeze after days
of unapologetic heat from rifle fire
and body bags, that moment the lilac leaves
imperceptibly shiver as honey suckle
begins to drift across the fallen porch,
as he sits at the edge of a fragrant listening.

Eyes open to confirm that he's not fallen,
not caught, not captured, but at a loss
for giving any kind of directions
on how to find him, hostage to a revelry,
still sitting next to a young woman
who believes that he is sitting there,
as his face begins to shatter into
the last moments of what can't be happening.

Coat draped over a three-legged chair.
Folded into grief, coat with a soul
waiting for rescue, waiting for one arm,
then the other, then to button a body closed.

To Catch a Bullet

Deep in deciduous forest
people stay hidden.

The Polish Officer Corp is still hiding
eighty years later in the Katyn Forest
Though only the Soviet archivists know where.

Autumn oaks get pushy.
Never cut back, they grow
too close to the house.

Acorns come knocking,
ricocheting off the metal roof.
Sometimes wildly loud.

Thrashed by a rough gust, someone
ducks to avoid automatic gunfire.

A friend on the next road,
who sold all his guns decades ago
bought a pistol the other day.

He said I needed to buy
 a 12-gauge pump-action shotgun.

The very sound of cocking
is enough to scare off most intruders.
and once the trigger is pulled,

I won't need to worry about my aim
or about catching a bullet.

Even with the front door closed,
the warmth of fall sunlight
slips in and curls once about the room.

His wife said they only need five bullets
and three are for the horses.
Better to stay hidden
In a house surrendering to forest.

Seventy Bodies Showing Signs of Torture

. . . death it waits for
for me in ordinary places where I
used to be safe.
                              -Anne Lindbergh

On a back road at fifty kilometers per hour,
dust a talcum shadow that powders
the rape seed and sunflowers. Slur of speed
and the only hope rising behind the steering wheel
is that no one's quick enough to get in the way
of the need to arrive at a vague somewhere
haunting this hour, or that they just kiss
the bumper and keep running or flying
firing at whatever moves.

Getting out of the way is another matter:
deer in the headlights, sliding over
the rusty hood, cracking the windshield,
or worse, breaking it and then the frantic
hooved kicking to nowhere. Most of the time
it's the speed of hope that forgets to ask
about the spare tire with its own nail to suffer,
the jack lost at the scene of the last flat,
where a bloated raccoon stared unflinchingly
out of the weeds at nothing in particular,
its four legs stuck straight into the cartoon air.

I watch in the rearview mirror something
roll to a stop. I turn the car around, drive back
slowly a hundred yards to where I heard the soft impact
of something against the door, as if a friend

might be placing a hand on the door latch
leaning in to tell me how a life can take
yet another wrong turn.

Door open, I reach down to pick up
what is flightless, place it lightly
on the seat next to me. It rocks
slightly on each turn of the drive home,
the bird so small it barely covers
the withered lifelines that cross my palm,
so green it should still be growing in this spring
even across these bomb-plowed fields
and forests splintered down to toothpicks.

I want hope to release its life into the air again,
but only see the ruby slash of a glittering
throat as the cool earth falls from my hand,
knowing the mad man, the generals,
could care less.

What can be said of the dead . . .

that they find themselves tired and lie down
in the middle of cobbled streets, as if all the facts
haven't yet reached them, and they will awaken
at any moment, as if only the wedged-together
reddish stones hold more solidly to their cold beliefs.

Yet there they are so innocent, some with their knees
half-drawn to their chests for a moment of fetal warmth,
hands folded, squeezed between their legs as a thin trickle
dampens their clothes as something dark drips from under
their disheveled hair, from their noses, a corner of their
mouths, as if they arranged themselves, or were marched
and told to wait right here, forever.

They are only trouble for the living who need explanations,
but are too busy themselves with dying and have no time
to tell these strangers, who once might have been friends,
to go somewhere else, to go over to the espresso cafe
where all the small round tables are overturned,
red and white umbrellas collapsed and torn,
to wait there. Perhaps a breeze will come along
to remind them of something they loved.

The living are too busy hiding another breath
in their own bodies, hoping that on this side of the street
it can't be found and taken away. Up ahead in the next
bullet-riddled doorway, another breath waits,
or behind a charred car, if they choose the right side;
but there's always that moment when they are too busy

talking to the dead to watch their backs, and then
they too press a hard ear against smooth stones,
joining the tired crowd on this street with their heads
all turned in the one direction only they can know.

This is what we say to the dead, that today we died
    with them,
joining the tired crowd of this street with their heads
all turned in the one direction only they can know.
This is what we say to the dead that today we died with
    them.

The Score

"Rocket tennis," how the apartments' tenants
keep score, keep perspective, laugh, save a bloody sliver
of sanity, so they don't throw open the scarred door
to run out into the debris strewn street,
believing they can win the game, leap the net,
shake hands, before they leave their city
with one more breath and their trophies in pieces.

At times it's background noise, the radio left on
in the kitchen. Sometimes the reception so broken,
it's a constant sizzle that they shout over to be heard.
They make up their own reports, asking yet again:
when did it start? when will it stop? when will their bodies
ever relax? always measuring the distance
and the incoming direction, maybe from beyond Gustav
    Street?
or farther out on Grimm Road? And when it's quiet
count who is still standing?

The distant tapping, each prisoner locked
in solitary confinement, communicating
with the broken-off corner of a concrete block,
tapping out a message. Only the basics:
why is she here and how long? has she been tortured?
is she getting enough food? are there cockroaches
swimming in her cold gruel? is the tapping a steady drip
into a metal pan or the rapping of a distant machine gun
that rushes into her dream of escape?

She stands in the living room paralyzed
hearing the windows rattle, the walls shiver,
the glass shattered into stilettos, everywhere
the air bleeding through the air, the odd chiming
of what can never be pieced back together,
a blinded kaleidoscope scattered across the floor.
Car alarms go off, a scream from the street,
a scream from next door, a scream frozen inside
her throat that she will never be able to spit out.
On either side of the net, "love" is zero.

After a Return to Abnormal

I go out to mow the yard,
to sweat and ache behind
the rupturing engine
balanced on wobbly wheels.
I landscape with holes.
Where else to begin
digging to Ukraine?

After that I build another room.
The drill sergeant orders me to chew
Through the wall before dinner.
The turnip soup floats
an armada of bristling spices.
I must eat the cold, lumpy mashed potatoes.

After that there's a sink full of dishes.
Wetted knives plan their ambush.
A hunger for secrets abounds.
Forks wound the water
till it's too murky to see the bottom.
Plates are the first to crack
under pressure to come clean.
They are set in the rack for a drier truth.

What happens after all this?
Thinner doors are found
for the starved.
Supper is always one orphan short.
Birds survive cats.

Cats survive themselves.
The dishes are stacked in cupboards.
The mowing stops. After the drought,
holes form large puddles. Removing
the landmine from around my neck,
I bend over to tie a bleeding shoe lace.

Piper

It came down to June 26th, AD 1284, in Hamelin.
It's an old story. It began as nothing serious, a few hungry
rats, skittering along the streets as if they owned them, coming

in from the cold to raid the winter grain supply until what
   remained was less
than expected. It was a day celebrating St. John and St. Paul,
close to the time of the pagan midsummer celebrations.

The date set by the town council for the Pied Piper,
master seducer, mesmerizing enchanter,
to arrive and clear the town of this infestation.

When the rats were led away and the Piper returned
to be paid, the town council refused.
The Piper donned his magician's high-pointed hat,

a rainbow-colored robe, and with that the children
followed him out of town never to return. Rumored, they were
led to a mountain lake and drowned, or sent off

to the east as slave labor, or left for a faraway land to escape
the early attack of the plague, or recruited for a crusade to win
back the Holy Land, or succumbing to St. Vitus Dance,

those unshakable, feverish gyrations that lasted days
with weeks of leaping, singing, hallucinating until exhausted,
their toy bodies spinning until they fell over and died.

A thousand years later another piper appears
without a flute, dressed in the dull glitter
and wretched dreams of empire. He doesn't remember

Hamelin's plea, the anguish of a corroded brass plaque
mounted on an ancient town wall: *One Hundred Years
Have Passed. Where Are Our Children?*

This piper doesn't mesmerize, he orders, he sneers, he
commands, he threatens, he devours, he dictates, he executes.
He rides in screaming his explosive glee,

he rides in on darkened "Z-striped" tanks, he dances
on the back of Zergs until so many have died
his feet are not dirtied by touching the ground

as he searches for more children to satisfy his hunger.
Clear out the preschools, the kindergartens,
the hospital birth rooms, daycare centers,

herd the little ones into buses and trucks, drive them
deep into a deeper frozen country. He claims this is mercy
to shield children from his Special Military Operation

that levels villages and cities, murders their parents
or leaves them crushed, crazed, crying without
hope as he swallows their children whole.

Nine Lives

A childhood game, hot potato.
Sitting in a sandbox, opposite a friend in each corner,
they throw something back and forth:

plastic bucket, rubber ball, instead of a hot potato,
and this time it's called a hand grenade.
How do they decide that it has exploded,

which one of them will leap backwards
out of the sandbox, arms and legs thrown
upward and outward, a human asterisk,

depends on who wants most to be a hero.
Heroes die first.
Their shrapnel-shredded flesh more real

than a scraped elbow or knee. Exactly
how many times can they die before dinner
can't be counted.

The Children

Cold, the boys start a fire out in the field
just beyond the cratered road that parallels the beach.
One boy empties into the conflagration a cigarette package

that holds shiny brass cartridges. The children run
screaming and diving for cover as the first bullet fires
into the fire further inflaming their raging hearts.

In quick succession the rest of the bullets whine and ricochet
spreading the flames over the pitted sand leaving only fading
embers. The children, amazed at hearing only the hiss

of receding waves, stand and brush off their
knees–this time the sweep of history stayed
far out at the charred edges of a blackened sea.

Brotherly Love

1

In 1994, the Budapest Memorandum stated that Ukraine
    would give up
its nuclear arsenal in exchange for a commitment from
    Moscow

"to respect the independence and sovereignty and existing
    borders of Ukraine."

2

Soldiers shoot dead at his home, a Ukrainian conductor
who refused to take part in a concert in occupied
    Kherson.

A Ukrainian soldier beheaded
    with a cheap kitchen knife.

A POW is shot dead
For shouting, *Slava Ukraini.*

A prisoner of war is castrated.

3

The words are not gone, just too frightened to be spoken.
What lies along the side of the road is bloated from
    summer heat.

.

Patrol

Air a steel door, fingers arthritic hinges,
They walk through, cinch khaki coats
Closer to their rusting bodies.
The road oiled with ice
Surrendering every direction but horizontal.
Steps accumulate. Are they saying goodbye
As they must or is it too early?
Are they saying hello
But too soon for a full accounting?
Kalashnikovs jumpy in their arms.

At every downturn, variations of gray
And brown against horizons of whiteness.
Surely the colors of grief.
Autumn abandoned to winter.
Surely the colors of uncertainty.
So many unkempt promises unkept,
Only cling to once bright betweens.

Hills hold the valley.
Slopes fold one way then back the other.
The wind bullies the desiccated leaves.
White scuffs of snow trail across the ice,
Descent not a choice. They are blown
across the frozen creek.
They keep walking. Quick to stop and listen.
Quick to aim. Quick to stand down
And breathe again. Water mindlessly
fulfills the widening banks.

The mottled brown gravel cut by time
Shuffles a losing hand of shells and fossils.
Then back to the ridge, staring over
Their shoulders as the water turns away.

Later bodies are resurrected from coats.
It's the coats that walk away. The search
Continues. A pair of glasses, dry socks,
all that hint of being rescued.

Swallowing the Mystery

1

The elliptical leaves of the cottonwood
on the other side of the garden, each is attached
to a three-sided stem, each positioned to catch
the slightest breeze, so in the late light of a sultry

evening, they paddle leisurely through the air,
going nowhere, but leaving a spangled wake
as he limps into the shadows of all of his mistakes.
He has seen in photographs and museums, other, larger

spade-shaped paddles carved from exotic woods,
decorated with spirals, that ever-tightening
incised circle that could be a warning of mythic
backwater whirlpools, or in the ever-opening

unravelling cosmos. Each a drowning,
each leaving him gasping,
universes upon universes as cosmologists
model soap bubbles building on

soap bubbles, and who knows what's headed for
the drain with no one yet dry behind the ears.

2

Around the mouth of the Norway lobster, not just
a new species but a new phyla is discovered clinging
on cilia, living on the scraps of meals, not
a millimeter long and in their asexual stage

they look like a field of swaying mummies, and so
for years on restaurant plates what is devoured
is the unknown and the filling satisfaction. This time
he wants more, and this time in the hills

along the Dnieper River, the fields all the way down
to the Black Sea, the bulldozers and backhoes begin
to drop their steel blades to bare hidden universes,
to surrender theories of origins: from mass graves,

he wants to know each end, the trajectory of each
    jawbone,
every curved femur of space, the caliber of every black
    hole,
he wants to know that afternoon, that evening,
he wants to know what species, which war, which
    universe.

Relearning the Alphabet

1   This alphabet doesn't have a "Z",
maybe a "Zed." In the central Russian city of Kazan,
60 children and staff stand in three-feet-deep
snow to form a giant human "Z".
In front of their concrete-block hostel,
they hold their raised hands, forming
an unbreakable victory chain that is
already broken as they stand under
a sky of heavy gray lies. The city of Kyiv
did not surrender in three days.

The flat space under each dorm window
That surrounds the courtyard, is painted
an anemic red as if the bleeding
was about to stop, or a muddy yellow
as if there is nothing left but to bury itself
deeper, or a slimy green that chokes spring fields
that are smothered in black ashes called snow.

2   Emblazoned on sweatshirts along sidewalks,
in shopping malls, on bus shelters and stone walls,
on car bumpers, street lampposts, on car doors
and sides of vans, on the lapels of every corrupt politician,
soon all words must begin and end with "Z".
"Z" the only patriotic letter left to tell the story.
"Z" clearly visible on the wreckage
along miles of muddy Ukrainian roads.
There is no room left for any other letter.

"War makes you funny, doesn't it?"

—Ukrainian soldier in Bakhmut

1   If there's an emergency, or just to say hello, there's no longer a home to call home. In those early days everything that was supposed to never happen, happened, which was just another thing that was supposed to happen when all fell into or was thrown down a rabbit hole. Depending on what he thought he was waiting for, which was almost never what was supposed to happen and then never happened, but then something would come along, enough to distract him, or cause him to forget, or maybe he was waiting and hoping to forget, or he could claim he never had a choice, still it was all going to happen or not happen no matter what he did or didn't do, so he doesn't wear a helmet or a flak jacket, any moment life is a lifetime, death an instant.

2   A house grabs a coat and runs down its own hallway, throwing open the back door, running out of itself, maybe a cousin to sea cucumbers that turn themselves inside out when threatened, and then jettison their own internal organs, but then no one is targeting it with a submersible missile. The house sees that the garage door is open and jumps into the driver's seat of the parked SUV. The house's second story is packed in the back seat. It looks through the side mirrors before backing out. Mascara applied around its front windows. Maybe no one will notice that an unlicensed house is careening through a war zone trying to keep its roof on in hope of escape before the missiles rain down. Its back windows are making sure there is nothing blocking its panicked retreat as it careens forward.

3   A house is not a home and to assume that a home is a house is a foolish confusion. Speeding past the charred and gutted cars, past the knee-deep rubble from once high-rise apartments, past the splintered linden trunks and leafless branches, through the destruction of destruction until there is only dust and tire tracks. The side mirrors are blinded by a wall of meat as the emergencies pile up on the side of the road until the bodies are cold and the living are desperate to forget.

4   The house can't cross the half-destroyed bridge that leads out of town. The self-driving SUV seizes its chance and crosses the bridge. The house sets itself down near the bridgehead, closes its windows, pulls the curtains closed, time to be a home again, and wait for the night to descend into rubble.

Water Wounds

At first it was dishwater as his hands
caressed the plate's chipped circle
        of hunger. Then he dared the fork's tines,
        thinking of today's skewered rat
from under the barn's rotten hay
squealing at the end of a pitch fork.

Only half-afraid of the knife's story,
but then the weather changed,
        clouds swept in, legions of porcelain islands
        in oceans of Delft blue. White birds
soared between his fingers.
His palms make dizzying dives,

suffering a wet vertigo. The birds begin to panic
as he chases them with the drying motions
        of a dish towel. He is a millworker,
        machinist, soldier, watching a foot,
a finger, an arm, work its way through
the machinery of the world without him.

Rorschach faces blot the dirt,
imprinted on walls, staining sidewalks—
        alone to imagine his body back.
        All he can think: after this, after that,
he pulls ten fingers from the dirty water,
the last cup placed in the dish drainer.

For Those Who Stay Behind

1

Night, smoke blows in through the east window.
Cowering below the sill, he holds his breath
as if under water, recalling the future wave
that will wash him back up onto the beach

when he was a child,
where his bucket and shovel were dropped
recalling a summer that will never happen again
as the whistling ends and the shells fall,

before he can ever begin trenching a moat and raise
a white gull feather of surrender. He pulls the sash closed,
thinks about closing the woodstove vents, hopes the wind
changes direction, and forgets how many died today.

2

He opens the west window
now that the north one is a smoky casualty.
It's spring as if that makes a difference
to the manufacturers of arms and legs:

gun sights for the blinded,
triggers for the fingerless,
grenade launchers for the armless.
He wants a window open to hear

the spring frogs shouting their charge.
Frogs take up the call in the thousands,
so patriotic that they can't hear anything else.
Geese drag their winter-wounded chevrons.

Surrender made inaudible by frogs
fighting to the death. Is there any other way?
Smoke again, window closed.
He sits on the floor alone to himself.

Escape

Lately, my rut has grown deep.
In a way, I'm just spinning my wheels.
I do endless revising. Revisions of revisions
of revisions as if another layer of bandages
will heal the wounds. I'm heading toward
an old beginning, as the whistles blow,
and the trench parapets are climbed,
to charge across no man's land
to be lost under another carpet of bodies.

I'm not writing anything new,
And when I feel that way, Stephane Mallarme
tells me "Everything in the world exists
to end up in a book," so I sit down
and keep writing, listening to the wheels spin
deeper until the axles are locked in the mud
of all these sticky words that will never firm up
so I can drive away and never look back,
but I know I can't put the pen down just to head
for the next fold in the landscape
where I've never been.

But then Mark Doty whispers, "Every poem's/
half erased." and with that the rpms max out,
the accelerator pedal flat against the metal,
mud rooster-tailing in the rearview mirror
the car begins to lurch forward
and I can barely hear him whisper
over the engine's over-taxed whining,

"God, my dear . . ./is in the damages:/
aren't we always, if we're lucky,/
ruined into knowledge?" and I take
a deep breath as the muddy
ground erupts around me into
the bloom of bullets and brown orchids.

Peace

1

One side of every locked door is exile.
He throws his keys down.
Opposite walls embrace the executed
and the executioner.
He could keep walking,
propelled through proclamation,
propaganda, prophecy,
all the lies of power
hidden in twilight.
He will return to the intersection
of these walls to the ring of conspiracy
that locks him in a looted room.

2

The thud of a throttled brass clapper
An unexploded shell.
The church of St. Sebastian
No longer tolls his demise.
A statue is all that is left.
No one walking in front
or behind him hears
the sharpening fire as it scrapes
its way along concrete block
along the doors of abandoned cars,
this jangle a dull tune married
to the sidewalk.
Slippery as pools of blood,
flags snap to attention.

3

If he passes through the wall
and opens something
on the other side, perhaps
whatever he doesn't find here,
the keys hit harder before falling
and are lost in the tainted dirt.

4

It's too late, the way he walks without
a backward glance, past the faceless
pain of so many statues.
Boulevards lined with crumbling heroes
raising rusty swords to gut the stained air.

5

The orange streaked surface
reminds him of an autumn sunset
as he throws the keys across
the polluted Dnieper River, where the half-
submerged traffic of tires make dull turns
between floating vodka bottles
crowded with unread messages. They hit
a factory's sooted wall igniting sparks.
The door opens to a country on fire.

6

He throws the key ring
with its mangy rabbit's foot
to her, *always* and *never* triumphant.
She picks up the mangled glitter
as bullets ricochet off
the wall and pass through
into another occupied country
where she has always lived
under house arrest.

EPILOGUE

Remaining Remote

How many televisions were shot today?
How many televisions stepped on land mines
And limped home dragging shattered screens.
How many were carried on stretchers

To be saved or dumped at a landfill.
How many were missiled into hundreds of pieces.
How many were buried in collapsed apartment
Buildings, left longing for sofas crowded with eyes open.

He picks up the remote and it rejects him,
No, reviles him, refusing to display channels
That are mostly still too wet and red.
Screens smeared beyond comprehension.

The remote is a gun firing blanks
As the door is being kicked down.
The remote demands that he keep
His hands raised above his head.

Lost Ordnance

The first shovelful alive and rich.
I'm down on my knees breaking clods
with my hands; cool and smeared
across my palms, clouding my fingernails,
a damp earth that knows its time.
Standing again, I drive the shovel's blade
with a boot, hit something hard:
a muffled ring. It happens a second time.

I begin carefully to dig, remembering
the mid-river sandbar one dry spring
on the Nekar River a few years after the war.
Staring into rippled shocks of light,
I saw the black outline of a machine gun
exposed by the retreating water. Too young,
I couldn't swim the current to save it.

Those summers outside Heidelberg,
in the many-feet-thick fortifications
overgrown by sapling pines, it was there
I played my death over and over,
at one jagged blown hole or another,
on top of the parapet or in an empty
gun emplacement, my cheek finding
the carpet of moss, and somehow
my body jumping up to rehearse

the charge again. It didn't matter which
side I was on, the dying was so easy.

Around the perimeter, I dug up
spent shell casings that had hardly aged,
arranging their calibers
along bullet-riddled concrete ledges.
I'd toss their dirt-packed shiny brass into the air,
the filth of old battles dusting my clothes.

Not far off the groomed hills,
where one slope bowed into another,
as if they really did go on beyond
the entrance of white columns,
the fluted marble pillared against
a roof of engraved sky where words
fell one letter at a time on upturned eyes.
The surrounding flags streaked their colors
through wind, reminders of where
once they left and then arrived across
all those fields flowing with white crosses,
stars, and crescents, as if the most
important things we do are done over
and over. Holding my father's hand,
walking the perfect rows, looking for
no one name among the many, he was
surprised not to find his own battle weary
orders to hold his position fading.

On weekends, I'd see through the car's rain-
flecked back window, fields of bomb craters
turned upside down in streaming lenses of rain.
Still the craters filled with water,
working themselves into weed-choked
ponds where frogs exploded into a new season.

Through Weinheim and Ludwigshofen,
couples in shorts and sandals strolled arm
in arm, behind baby carriages and dogs
straining leashes, as if it were normal
to pass buildings with just one wall standing,
rooms crowded with sky, under eaves
with corners gouged out, stone and bricks
scribbled with the graffiti of shrapnel.

I work the shovel slowly now,
an ocean, a continent of time away,
feeling for the hidden edges, wanting to
loosen without jarring, knowing
of grenades, lost ordnance, that missed
their wars, their seed slow to detonate
in others' gardens and backyards,
where other children play
at the dead center of day.

Walter Bargen has published 27 books of poetry including: *My Other Mother's Red Mercedes* (Lamar University Press, 2018), *Until Next Time* (Singing Bone Press, 2019), *Pole Dancing in the Night Club of God* (Red Mountain Press, 2020), *You Wounded Miracle*, (Liliom Verlag, 2021), *Too Late to Turn Back* (Singing Bone Press, 2023), and *Radiation Diary: Return to the Sea* (Lamar University Press, 2023). He was appointed the first poet laureate of Missouri (2008-2009). His awards include: a National Endowment for the Arts Fellowship, Chester H. Jones Foundation Award, and the William Rockhill Nelson Award. He currently lives outside Ashland, Missouri, with his wife and too many formerly feral cats.

This project was made possible, in part, by generous support from the Osage Arts Community.

Osage Arts Community provides temporary time, space and support for the creation of new artistic works in a retreat format, serving creative people of all kinds — visual artists, composers, poets, fiction and nonfiction writers. Located on a 152-acre farm in an isolated rural mountainside setting in Central Missouri and bordered by ¾ of a mile of the Gasconade River, OAC provides residencies to those working alone, as well as welcoming collaborative teams, offering living space and workspace in a country environment to emerging and mid-career artists. For more information, visit us at www.osageac.org

Osage Arts Community